香港國際詩歌之夜 2017
INTERNATIONAL POETRY NIGHTS IN HONG KONG

編輯 Editors

北島 Bei Dao

柯夏智 Lucas Klein

宋子江 Chris Song

犁田白鷺

馬克・卓狄尼

EGRET IN A PLOUGHED FIELD

MARK TREDINNICK

《犁田白鷺》
馬克・卓狄尼 著

封面影像：北島

國際統一書號（ISBN）：978-988-237-046-3

出版：中文大學出版社
香港 新界 沙田・香港中文大學
傳真：+852 2603 7355
電郵：cup@cuhk.edu.hk
網址：www.chineseupress.com

Egret in a Ploughed Field
By Mark Tredinnick

Cover Image: Bei Dao

ISBN: 978-988-237-046-3

Published by The Chinese University Press
The Chinese University of Hong Kong
Sha Tin, N.T., Hong Kong
Fax: +852 2603 7355
E-mail: cup@cuhk.edu.hk
Website: www.chineseupress.com

Printed in Hong Kong

目錄 Contents

馬克・卓狄尼
Mark Tredinnick

中文翻譯：宋子江、鄭政恆

Egret in a Ploughed Field

At the close of day I watch an egret
nail a soft landing in a ploughed field and earth
The shallow sky. The ground is scoured where she falls, a soul
Turned, like a pocket, inside out, and the bird wanders
the black rows, scoring them loosely with its one bright
note.

She makes an inverse music, it seems to me,
plucking the furrows
For what they may yield, an improvised notation
That erases itself writing itself down, singing the earth back
silently
into the belly of a bird, a reverie

In negative, which wakes the dawning dark
all the way back to its beginning again. The bird's random
waltz
Down unwalled streets goes on—this little
Night music, these white field notes that pull up day's ends
by the roots
and leaf out the night—

Until the darker music, furloughed

                    here by day, swells and the bird fades, swallowed

By what she'd divined. And she leaves the darkness more

    luminously dark

Around the hole she cuts in it, flying blind

the ploughed field home to roost.

犁田白鷺

白天將盡，我看著一隻白鷺
輕輕降落，釘在犁田泥土上
天空淺淺的。她降落的地面都抹刷乾淨了，一具靈魂
反轉，猶如一個口袋，裏朝外。白鷺遊蕩在
黑色田畦上，用疏落亮白的音符來譜曲

在我看來，她在創造背反的音樂
鈎拔著犁溝
為了它們的產出。這種即興的記譜法
抹去自己書寫的自己，歌唱著大地，默默地把它
唱回白鷺的腹腔裏，一次夢幻

在負片裏喚醒破曉時分的黑暗
又把它送回原初。白鷺隨意跳著華爾茲
跳進沒有圍牆的街道上——一段短短的
夜曲，一串白色的音符，把白天的盡頭連根拔起
讓葉子開出黑夜——

直到更暗的音樂，讓白天暫時解僱
到這裏，直到它膨脹。鳥兒褪色

吞沒在神聖化之中。她把黑暗留在切離的洞口
留下更有亮澤的黑暗，盲盲飛過

梨田家巢。

Catullus, at dusk, heartbroken and lustful, tries his hand at haiku

You crashed my house. You
Smashed my household gods. So where
Am I now you've gone?

卡圖魯斯，黃昏
心碎了，色心起
生手寫俳句

你拆了我的房子。你
摔了我家的神主牌。那麼
你已離去，我在何方？

House of Thieves

I live in a house of thieves.
They steal my toast. They steal
My time. They steal my mornings
And they steal my nights. They steal the best of me,

And they steal the worst,
until I do not know how much is left of me
And what it's any good for. But I'd be no other man than this.
This looted self, blessed by theft,
this harbour for love's worst scoundrels.

賊窩

我住在一個賊窩裏。
他們偷走我的吐司。他們偷走
我的時間。他們偷走我的早晨
他們偷走我的夜晚。他們偷走最好的我，

他們偷走最壞的我，
直到我不知道自己還剩下幾多
剩下的用處幾何。但是我只做自己，不要做別人。
這個被洗劫一空的我，得到偷竊的保祐，
這個港灣，愛之最不堪。

The Kingfisher

For Maureen Harris

And so each bird throws the idea of herself
ahead of herself, up the river—
A line of spiritual thought without a sinker—
And flies after it. As if the actual could ever hope to reel the
ideal in. But so it is
That awareness of the Azure Kingfisher—a dark electricity,
a plump
Trim elegance of intent—reaches you on the riverbank
that last warm Sunday of autumn, split seconds
Before the bird; so that when she passes you at light speed,
her name
is already a bright blue phrase on your tongue, is already
the unresolved cadence of your second self.

藍翠鳥

給毛林・哈里斯

每一隻鳥兒都把自我的意念
投向自我的前方，河上——
一列心靈思緒，無一下沉——
飛蟲尾隨。彷彿真實有望捲收空想。而這就是
那隻藍翠鳥的意識——一道黑電，一次飛墮
意向有種修束的優雅——觸及河岸上的你
秋天最後一個暖和的週日，倏瞬
於鳥兒跟前；當她以光速飛過你跟前，她的名字
早已是舌頭上亮藍色的片語，早已是
第二個自我懸而未決的頓挫。

Lotus Pond

For Sarah

If you want heaven, start in mud.
                    Begin transfiguration
Where you're stuck. Take your pilgrimage standing
Up to your ankles in sludge. And if the ground binds
                    and if your boots stick, and if you step
Out of them when you set off; if the odour
On a summer's day, when the water ebbs, is noisome
                    where you begin, so much more pure

Your thoughts will be when they flower,
                    so much sweeter the garden's scent when
You breathe it in, so much more like birdsong
Your voice when you begin at last to speak. Start underwater
                    if you want the sky. Start in the abject
Underworld, if you want the lighted Earth; start among
The throng of ears that cannot hear. Sink in detritus, seed in
                    the strife that your life, and every life,

Falls into now and then: Serenity
                    springs from squalor; love is only love if it
Can bear the badlands out. These wastes—good for nothing
    more substantial—

Bloom light and outshine day. The lotus pond,
                    a repurposed wetland well south of its days,[1]
Is a perfect picture, empty, of the imperfection of your soul,
Helplessly in love with the vulgate particulars
                              of the secondhand world; in flower,

The pond is your Buddha self
                at her ease; the Christ of St Thomas[2] come down
From the cross. Freedom starts, but refuses to stay, in want;
Literature takes its first steps in slur and slurry.
                              Put down roots where no one
Else can, in the compost of loss, in the suspect terrain
Of the only life you may ever get to grow in.
                              Nothing is wrong for long

And hope cannot stay lost,
                              if beauty can walk from the wreck,
And the lotus can raise heaven
                              from the dreck and the dross.

1 *well south of its days*: "South of My Days," Judith Wright.

2 *Christ of St Thomas*: the Cross of St Thomas features a lotus.

荷塘

給莎拉

如果你要天堂，就從淤泥起步吧。
　　　　　　　開始顯容吧，
就在你裹足不前的地方。你立足朝聖
泥濘上及腳踝。如果地面捆綁
　　　　　　　如果靴子黏稠，如果你
脱靴而去，如果夏季
一天裏的香味，當池塘的水退去，就是惡臭
　　　　　　　你起步的地方，就更純潔了。

當它們開花，你的想法就出現了
　　　　　　　當你呼吸，花園香味
更甜美了。當你最終決定開口説話
你的聲音更像鳥兒歌唱了。如果你要天空
　　　　　　　就從水底起步吧。如果你要
照亮的大地，就從悲涼的地府起步吧，就從
那簇聽不見的耳朵起步吧。沉沒在腐壞之中，把種子
　　　　　撒播在紛爭之中，你的生命，每一個生命

都不時墮入其中：寧靜
　　　　　　　從骯髒中噴湧；愛是為愛，如果它
經受得住荒瘠之地。這些糟粕—— 一無是處——

盛放光芒，蓋過白日。這個荷塘

一片改變用途的濕地，它時日中的南方[1]

是一張完美的圖畫，空空的，畫中是你不完美的靈魂

無助地愛上了二手世界裏

通行的細節。花開之時

荷塘就是你的佛陀自我

她的自在。聖托馬斯基督從十字架上[2]

降臨。自由起步了，但是拒絕停下來，有所缺失

文學在污點和泥漿中踏出第一步

扎根於失去的有機肥料之中

沒有其他事物可以做到。在這可疑的地帶

唯一的生命可以讓你生長其中。

沒有甚麼會錯得很久

希望也不會一直迷失，

假若美麗可以走出頹唐

假若荷花可以從糟粕和浮渣中

舉起天堂

1　「時日中的南方」語出澳洲詩人朱迪斯・萊特。

2　聖托馬斯的十字架樣子像荷花。

Wrack

So why is it when I wake
                                        beside this Cornish sea, my tongue
Is as tired as it only gets to be, lost in deep,
Prolonged and riotous discourse with thee? My sleep
Has been as eloquent, it seems,
              as the breeze that trafficked my window all night,
As busy as the sea at her six-metre rise and fall across the
    shingle
Of the shore. Seabirds wake me late, stealing back in
    strident sunlight
Songs—sea shanties, lullabies—that slaked me while I slept.
                              And the dreams in my mouth on waking—
Though I remember none of their sweet filibuster, none
Of the exquisite slow coming to so many disparate points—
My dreams are salted
                                                  with you and fragrant
With longing for the sea
That tossed me in her bed and used my tongue
Like bladder wrack and left me shipwrecked
At half-eleven in her lap.

失事

當我醒來

　　　在康尼什海邊，為何我的舌頭

只會累成如斯模樣，迷失於彼此

唇舌之間。深刻，綿長且放浪。我的睡眠

似乎一場雄辯

　　　猶如微風整夜貫穿窗口

忙碌得就像海升高了六米，又落在

海岸邊的卵石上。海鳥遲遲叫早，偷回扎耳的

陽光之歌——船夫之歌，搖籃曲——沉睡時為我

　　解渴。

　　　　　　　　　半醒時夢掛在嘴邊

記不起任何甜蜜的拖延，細膩地慢慢醒來時

記不起任何迥異的細節——

你讓我的夢

　　　有了海腥味；讓我的夢有了芬芳

對海的渴望

把我扔到她的床上，利用過我

如墨角藻般的舌頭，讓我失事於她

十一點半的腿縫間

Your Skin

My love, I miss your skin.
No one has known it as I have known it.
No one has loved it as I have loved it. No one has held your body
In their hands and taken it with their whole imperfect life as I have
Taken it and made it my bed.
No one has travelled your skin—that
Satin skein of sense and sin, the nakedness you wear like the blackest
Dress at the brightest ball—as I have travelled your skin in sex and
Sleep and mornings and broken-up regretful streets.
My love, I miss your skin.
My tongue is a new language your body has learned in silence to speak
In violent cries the size of Canada and sighs that fell the angels
From the fathoms of the skies;
my tongue is versed and cursed in you
And steeped in the fragrant reek of all the time reversed in you; my want is

Undressed and rehearsed; led out at dawn, my lust is
tortured and confessed
At the unholy unrelenting form of you;
so damage me and make me pay,
And teach my tongue again to say the only words a mouth
that's known
Your skin would care to pray:
Sarah's godly neck, her good for nothing
Waist, her sullen nipples, an orchard in rain, the brothel of
her breasts,
Her lips. But ah, my love,
I miss your skin. My thirst, a thirsty year
Drought, is slaked in the Midsummer lake of you, and my
hunger
Is a wolf at large in the winter wastes of you.
No one has lived in a holy rage
Of hope for you as I have lived and died and lived again and
died
A hundred nights with you in my private worship of your
thighs,
Of your waist, of your overcast eye,
You are the scripture I would strip

From the liturgies and pillage from the pulpits and turn in
    my mouth
Into a gospel of profanity, debauchery and fire.
                                        I wish you were the forest floor
So that I might sink my roots in you and turn your skin to
    rain.
If you were the river, I would gladly drink you dry and
    drown in
The casual pleasure of drinking you down.
                                        My fingers are an army
Of lust and you their battleground, and your skin is a field
I will never conquer but never stop laying siege to. My love,
I miss your skin.
                                        And all metaphors aside, I want your skin,
My love—for itself and for the uncanny and chaotic, the
    loyal
And unquenchable self it contains, like the secret the world
Wakes to discover again each day;
                                        I want to use you thoroughly,
My love, to wear your skin in and and to wear it right out
    again,

Under the unrelenting tenderness of my affection. I want
you
To know I will never be done, my love, with wanting your
skin
And making you pay in pleasure and pain for what my want
has cost.

愛的肌膚

我的愛，我想念你的肌膚。

　　　　　　　　　　　　沒有人如我這般熟悉你。

沒有人如我這般愛你。沒有人如我這般用你的手

抱起你的身體，沒有人如我這般接受你完整

而不完美的生活，把你當成床鋪

　　　　　　　　沒有人如我這般在你的肌膚上游弋

感官罪孽錦緞糾纏，你穿上赤裸猶如在最明亮的舞會中

穿上最深黑的衣裝。做愛時、沉睡時、還是走在

一片頹喪和懊悔的街上時，我都在你的肌膚上游弋

　　　　　　　　　　　　我的愛，我想念你的肌膚

我的舌頭是一門新的語言，你的身體在沉默中學會了講

暴戾的叫喊，大得像加拿大；歎息讓天使

從天空的深淵墮落；

　　　　　　　　我的舌頭在你身上編成詩句，落下詛咒

沉溺在時間的芬芳腐臭裏，一切時間在你身上轉逆；我

　　的缺失

被脱光，被排演；我的情慾，黎明時分被帶走，被折

　　磨，被迫

在你不神聖、不念情的形相面前認罪

　　　　　　　　　那麼就摧毀我吧，讓我付出代價

再來教我的舌頭説出那些嘴巴認得的字詞

你的肌膚會在乎會祈禱的字詞

　　　　　　　　　　　莎拉的纖阿脖子，一無是處的

蠻腰，陰沉的乳頭，雨中果園，胸脯妓院

還有她的嘴唇。但是，啊，我的愛

　　　　　　　　　我想念你的肌膚。我的饑渴，饑渴

乾涸的一年，在你的仲夏之湖中得到解脱。我的飢餓

是你的嚴冬荒野上的一隻野狼

　　　　　　　沒有人如我這般活在一種神聖的暴怒中

暴怒源自對你的希望，如此活著又死去又復活又復死

一百個深夜與你一起，我私底下拜倒在你的大腿上

纖腰間，還有你陰沉的眼下

　　　　　　　　　你是一段經文，我會從宗教禮儀中

把你撕下，從講道台上把你搶奪，經過我的口舌

把你變成一部褻蕩惹火的福音

　　　　　　　　　　　　　　　　願你是一片林地

我就能把根伸入你，把你的肌膚變成雨水

如果你是一段河流，我會樂意地把你喝到乾涸，沉溺在

把你喝下去的樂趣中

　　　　　　　　　　　我的手指是一支情慾軍隊

而你就是他們的戰場，你的肌膚就是我永遠也無法征服

又永遠也無法停止圍攻的陣地。我的愛
我想念你的肌膚。

撇開所有隱喻，我渴求你的肌膚

我的愛——為了它自己，也為了它包涵的自我
詭秘、混沌、忠誠、無法熄滅的自我，就像這個世界
每天醒來都會發現的秘密

我要徹底地把你穿來脫去

我的愛，把你的肌膚穿在體內，又反過來穿在體外
帶著愛慕裏無情的溫柔。我要你
知道，我的愛，我永遠不會歇止渴求你的肌膚
我為此付出代價，也要你為此付出快樂和痛苦

The Ugly

After John Glenday, "The Ugly"

The future refuses the past,
And the way
Things seem is rarely how things are. The present
Is a stranger to itself.
The plants go on
The best way they know how, being
Themselves as well as they can manage
In the changing face
of things, becoming
The world (each is born to be), each after
Its own fashion.

What we love in the one we love
Is the life
No one else knows how to live. Our love is how
We tend that gift
Which is hers alone.
And so, if I say I love her as I love the future
That unsettles everything I thought I knew,
I hope you'll understand.
I love her as time

Loves the *Welwitschia mirabilis*—after the corpse
Flower, the stinky squid,

The vegetable sheep, the fourth
Ugliest plant,
In botanical minds, in the world—who sets two leaves,
Once every two
Thousand years, and rolls them
Like ragged swags along the desert's floor, and thrives
In fabulous disarray so long
Under the Namibian
Sun, her leaves splitting
And sweeping themselves into a mess in a corner,
We may as well call it forever.

If your love lasts so long
They'll be calling it
A miracle. Find in your heart, then; find
In the heart of the one
You love, what grows nowhere
Else; love it, that stranger, as the wise learn
To love the Leafless Rockwattle;
The *acacia alata*

(var. Biglandulosa), that crowd
Of thorns; the green bird flower; the small-
Leaved Mottlecah,

A fallen altocumulus, her flowers
Like black holes
At a disco. Wander the world, a pilgrim of hard places;
Plumb your own deep north,
Your farthest west, and find there,
Where they prosper, the unconforming,
The wasted saints,
The scholars of the other
Way, the fallen dervishes, forever
Finding their two or three left feet again,
The addicts of the edge,

And see if you can find the future
In their ancient
Eyes, and in their image divine your days: the candel-
Abra aloe, burning sea-cliffs
Into ballrooms; the spiked cabbage
Tree, its leaves hors d'oeuvres for elephants,

Its roots a balm
To calm chaotic minds; *euphorbia ingens*,
A pot plant grown gargantuan
On the run; and the royal poinsiana, red carpet
For a canopy,

Its pea-green seeds faux canapes
For kingfishers
And dollarbirds, for princes and paupers and thieves,
To ignore,
Its leaves a sleepy tracery of summer
Dreams. How we contradict ourselves is who
We are; how we die to what
We'd hoped to be and rise again
Strange to ourselves as the future
To the past. Love is our work, whatever shape
It wants to take
In time

醜陋

擬約翰・格蘭地〈醜陋〉

未來拒絕往昔
而事物的方式
似乎很少一如所是。此刻
是自身的陌生人
植物繼起
它們知到最佳的方式，成為
它們自己，而且它們可以應付
事物改變的
面貌，成為
世界（各自天生），各自跟從
自身的裝束。

我們愛所愛者的
是生命
沒有人知道如何生活。我們的愛就是
如何照管她獨自的
禮物。
所以，如果我說我愛她，一如我愛未來
就會擾亂我以為自己所知的一切
我希望你會明白。

我愛她，一如時間
愛百歲蘭——在屍花、
紡錘佛手菌、

殘雪草之後，排名第四
最醜陋的植物
在植物學的頭腦中，在世間——百歲蘭開出兩片葉
每兩千年
一次，翻捲
一如沿著沙漠地表上的破爛行囊，長久地
在驚人的雜亂中茁壯成長
在納米比亞的日光
之下，她的葉子裂開
又自我捲成一角狼藉
我們也把它叫做永恆

如果你的愛曠日持久
他們會把它叫做
奇蹟。那麼，在你的內心尋找；在你所愛的人的
內心中尋找不在別處
生長的事物；愛它，那個陌生人一如智者學習

愛無葉的金合歡樹；

　　翅枝

　　　　　　　　　金合歡，一堆

荊棘；綠鳥花；細葉

　　　　桉樹花，

　　墜落的高積雲，她的花

　　　　一如的士高裏的

黑洞。周遊世界，難行之地的朝聖者；

　　探測你自己的北部深處，

　　　　你西部最遠之處，到那裏尋找，

　　到他們繁盛的地方尋找，不隨俗

　孱弱的聖者

　　　另闢蹊徑的

　　　　學者，墮落的苦行僧，永遠

尷尷尬尬地站著

　　　　危險邊緣的入迷者，

　　然後看看你可否在他們

　　　　古老的眼睛裏

找到未來，或者從他們的形象猜測你的時日：南非

　　蘆薈，將海崖燃燒成

舞廳；穗狀花序的
澳洲朱蕉，葉子是大象的前菜，
它的根是香膏
鎮靜混亂的思緒；燭台樹，
忙個不停地
龐然生長的盆栽；鳳凰木，樹冠的
紅地毯，

青豆色種子，假的餐前薄餅
給翠鳥
和三寶鳥，給王子、窮人和盜賊
忽略了，
它的葉子是夏夢
睡意朦朧的窗花格。自相矛盾
我們正是如此；我們如此渴望
我們曾希望成為的自己，然後再次復活
對自己感到陌生，猶如往昔
之於未來。愛是我們的勞作，無論它
要以何種形態
存在於時光裏。

Lucy and the Tree

She never saw a tree she didn't need
                                to climb. Some things you have to see
Can only find you there. She needs loft, my girl.
Limbs A father's arms will do, but nothing beats
A tree. A birch, she's learned, will leave the distance
(Where it is) and make a garden grow
                                a sky. A decade old

Today, a digit for each syllable
                                of her name; still
In the lower branches of her years,
But already taller than her days, she's bright
With all the light she learns up there.
I think of how I couldn't find her
On the day I had to leave. At last, I heard her amber voice

Fall down from high up
                                where she leafed out
In the poplar's crown. *I'm teaching the tree to see*, she said.
And, ah, you are the summer
                                of my grief, my girl, as near to heaven
As I would ever hope to reach.
You teach my days to hope again. You coach
my forest heart to yield.

露絲與樹

她從不看她不用爬的
　　　樹。一些你不得不看的事物
只能夠找到你。她要到高處，我的女兒。
四肢，父親的手臂還可以，但沒甚麼比得上
一棵樹。她學到，白樺樹會離開遠方
（它的所在），讓一個花園生長出
　　　一片天空。今日

十歲，她名字的音節
　　　各有一個數字；依然
在她人生較矮的分支，
但已比她的年紀更高了，她在樹上認識光
她跟所有認識的光一同明亮。
　　　我想到我要離去的那天
如何找不著她。最終，我聽到她琥珀般的聲音

從高處墜落
　　　她在白楊的樹冠裏
長葉。「我在教樹觀看」，她說。
啊，你是我的憂傷的
　　　夏日，我的女兒，如此接近天堂

我一直希望自己可以抵達的地方。
你教我如此年紀仍會盼望。你教
我心之森林開枝散葉。

The Horse

For Lucy

Real drawing is a constant question,
is a clumsiness, which is a form
of hospitality towards what
is being drawn.
—John Berger

there is a landscape, veined, which only a child can see
or the child's older self, a poet…
—Adrienne Rich, "Dreamwood"

She's at a loss, my daughter, in the drawing
She makes, a girl and her horse, as a gift
For me—a frontispiece she pens,
Beside my name, which she inscribes
As if it were her own, on the first page
Of my new notebook:
                                        Freckles and a quandary
Upon her face; one foot in one camp,
The other in another. Her face asks
A question to which her body wants

An answer.

And beside her, a horse, and
It leans her way, the way she's drawn it,
This pony, infinitely tender, waiting for her,
The girl in the picture, to notice that she,
The girl with the pen, already has
What she always wanted, standing
At her side.

When I lived with her, she rode
Me sometimes; sometimes, though she's nine,
And is beginning to forget, she rides me still.
I have loved horses and ridden them, and
Every birthday and Christmas, knowing
Her hope was hopeless, she's asked for one,
Which never came.

We've loved horses together,
She and I, and her hope for horses was our
Love for each other, and I drew them
For her from The World of the Horse,
And from storybooks I gave her because
I couldn't give her a horse.

We loved each other
Many ways, but how we both loved horses
Was how we loved each other best.
If I tell you,
Then, we are the horse she's drawn, she and I,
Or that I am the horse and she is the girl,
You'll know why, and you'll understand
How her drawing cries my longing
For her, the way it sings her longing
For us.
Opening my journal, tonight, I see
The two of us, hopeful and kind and confused,
Wondering how we stand now and what
Will become of all we loved, and what will
Become of us.

Knowing, as children
Know—and drawings that are real—much
More than she knows, my girl has drawn
A question to which I—to which we—are
The answer in the horse's eye: *Yes*, I want
To tell her; *yes*.

What you long for, my love,
Stands beside you, a father beside his girl,
All you ever wanted, a horse that will not
Run, an answer more tender than time.
What you long
For longs for you, and even when you
Cannot see me, and you are not sure
I know, I know.
I stand beside you, my girl,
And I stood there all along, and I stand
Beside you ready, all the days of your life.

馬

給露絲

真正的繪畫是一恆常的提問，
一種不熟練，就是
對所繪畫之物
表達的一種款待形式。
——約翰・伯格

有一片風光，有紋理的，唯獨孩子能見
或小孩年老些的自我，一個詩人……
——艾德麗安・列治〈夢林〉

她茫然若失，我的女兒，她繪畫
一個女孩和她的馬，作為給我的
禮物。她把卷頭插畫
畫在名字旁邊，她把我的名字
題寫在新筆記本的扉頁
彷彿她題寫的是
自己的名字：
　　　　　　一臉雀斑
與為難；三心
兩意。她的臉孔

在詢問，對於這個問題，身體也想要
答案。

她的身邊有一匹馬
歪向一邊，她繪畫的姿勢使然。
這匹小馬無限溫柔，等著
畫中的女孩，又注意到
執筆的女孩，已經
一如所願，站立在
她那邊。

我跟她同住時，她有時
騎膊馬；有時，即使她九歲，
開始會忘記，她仍舊騎膊馬
我曾經愛馬和策馬，而
每個生日和聖誕，我知道
她的願望都是無望的，她要一隻馬
而馬沒有來。

我們曾經都愛馬，
她和我，她擁有馬的願望就是
我們彼此的愛。我為她而畫的馬
都是取材於《馬的世界》

以及我給她的故事書，因為
我不能給她一匹馬。
　　　　　　　　　　　　　我們愛彼此
有許多種方式，我們都愛馬
是我們愛彼此最好的方式。
　　　　　　　　　　　如果我告訴你
她和我，我們就是她畫的馬；
又或者我是那匹馬，她是那個女孩，
你就會知道為甚麼，你就會明白
她的繪畫如何呼喚出我對她的
思念，這幅畫如何唱出她對我們的
思念。
　　　　　　今夜，我打開日誌，看到
我們兩個都抱有希望，親切而困惑
好奇我們如何不變，我們
所愛的一切會如何，我們
又會如何。

　　知道，一如小孩
所知道——以及真實的畫——
比她所知道的更多。我的女兒畫了

一道問題，在馬的眼裏
答案是我，是我們。「是的」
我想告訴她，「是的。」
　　　　　　　　你所思念的，吾愛，
就站在你身邊，父親在女兒身邊。
你想要的一切，一匹不會跑的
馬，一個比時間更溫柔的答案。
　　　　　　　　　　你所思念的事物
也思念你，即使你
看不見我，你不肯定
我知道。我知道的。
　　　　　　我站在你身邊，我的女兒，
我一直站在那裏，在你身邊
隨時隨地，一生一世。

When the Panic

When the silence grows shrill in you and won't be said;
When the sadness grows deep like winter in you, but will

Not well; when the panic rises, like the past, and won't
Be shaken; when five years of untaken sleep become

A nightmare of doubt, a life in drought; when the fear
Wakes before you with the scissors in its hands; when

Hope becomes a harder case than you know how to make;
When the floor drops out from everything you thought

You were and meant and knew; when the world shrinks
Back to shibboleth and nothing peaceful anywhere knows

The letters of your name—I want you to remember this:
The panic passes, the fear will end; the pieces into which

Your days have frayed and fallen will become a life
Again, and it will be your own. You'll never get over

Any of this, but you will, without a doubt, get through.

You will stand glad under a winter moon and smell

The weather change and know that when you wake
It will be spring.
            and the years will have turned their faces
To all the light that's been falling your way from the start.

恐慌之時

當沉默在你身上變得刺耳而不能說，
當悲傷在你身上變得深沉如冬天，但

不會流湧；當恐慌冒現，一如往昔，無法
擺脫；當無休眠的五年成為

一場懷疑的惡夢，乾旱的人生；當恐懼
手執剪刀在你面前醒來；當

希望成為比你所知更艱難的立論；
當地板從一切你以為你所是、所在、所知

當中脫離；當世界退縮
到過時習俗，任何地方的和平都不知道

你名字的字母——我想你記得：
恐慌過後，恐懼也會結束；你的日子

磨損墜落而成的碎片，將會再次成為
生活，將會屬於你自己。你再也不會

克服它，但毫無疑問，你會挺過來的。
你會在冬月下保持高興，察覺到

天氣的變化，而且知道你醒來時
就會是春天。
　　　年歲會把臉轉向光芒
從一開始就落在你的路途上。

馬克・卓狄尼(澳洲),當代澳洲著名詩人、散文家,在澳洲各地學校教寫作,參加過澳洲、美國和英國等地的文學節。曾獲Montreal詩歌獎、Cardiff詩歌獎、Blake詩歌獎、Newcastle詩歌獎、Calibre散文獎。兩次獲頒澳洲國內的州長文學獎。他所著的地景回憶錄*The Blue Plateau*入選澳洲總理文學獎。2016年獲ACU詩歌獎;2017年獲Ron Pretty詩歌獎。

Mark Tredinnick (Australia) is a celebrated poet, essayist, and writing teacher. His honours include the Montreal and Cardiff Poetry Prizes, The Blake and Newcastle Poetry Prizes, two Premiers' Literature Awards, and the Calibre Essay Prize. *The Blue Plateau*, his landscape memoir, shortlisted for the Prime Minister's Prize. He travels and teaches widely, in schools and at festivals, through Australia and in the US and UK. In 2016 his poem "The Horse" won the ACU Poetry Prize; in March 2017, his poem "Panic Very Softly, Love" won the Ron Pretty Poetry Prize.

香港國際詩歌之夜 2017
International Poetry Nights in Hong Kong 2017

主辦單位 Organizers

香港中文大學文學院
Faculty of Arts, The Chinese University of Hong Kong
香港詩歌節基金會有限公司
Hong Kong Poetry Festival Foundation Limited

協辦單位 Co-organizers

香港中文大學中國文化研究所
Institute of Chinese Studies, The Chinese University of Hong Kong
香港中文大學出版社
The Chinese University Press
香港大學美術博物館
The University Museum and Art Gallery, The University of Hong Kong
香港大學文學院
Faculty of Arts, The University of Hong Kong
香港科技大學賽馬會高等研究院
Jockey Club Institute for Advanced Study, Hong Kong University of Science and Technology
香港科技大學人文學部
Division of Humanities, Hong Kong University of Science and Technology
廣州時刻文化傳播有限公司
Moment Communications
活字文化
MoveableType Legacy (Beijing) Co., Ltd.
當當
DANGDANG

贊助 Sponsors

中國會 The China Club
北京匡時國際拍賣有限公司 Beijing Council International Auction Co., Ltd.
先鋒公益基金會 UCF Charity Foundation Limited
卓爾書店 the zall bookstore
斑馬谷文化發展有限公司 Zebra Valley Culture Development
馮鑫牟希文夫婦 Feng Xin (Larry) and Mu Xi Wen (Maggie)
蓮華書院 Lianhua Academy